Anonymous

The Pocumtuc Housewife

a guide to domestic cookery, as it is practiced in the Connecticut Valley

Anonymous

The Pocumtuc Housewife
a guide to domestic cookery, as it is practiced in the Connecticut Valley

ISBN/EAN: 9783337092184

Printed in Europe, USA, Canada, Australia, Japan

Cover: Foto ©Andreas Hilbeck / pixelio.de

More available books at **www.hansebooks.com**

The

Pocumtuc Housewife

A Guide to Domestic Cookery

A Choice Conserve

❀ ❀ ❀

THE Fruit of Experience freshly gathered from Elderly
Lips, now preserved in print

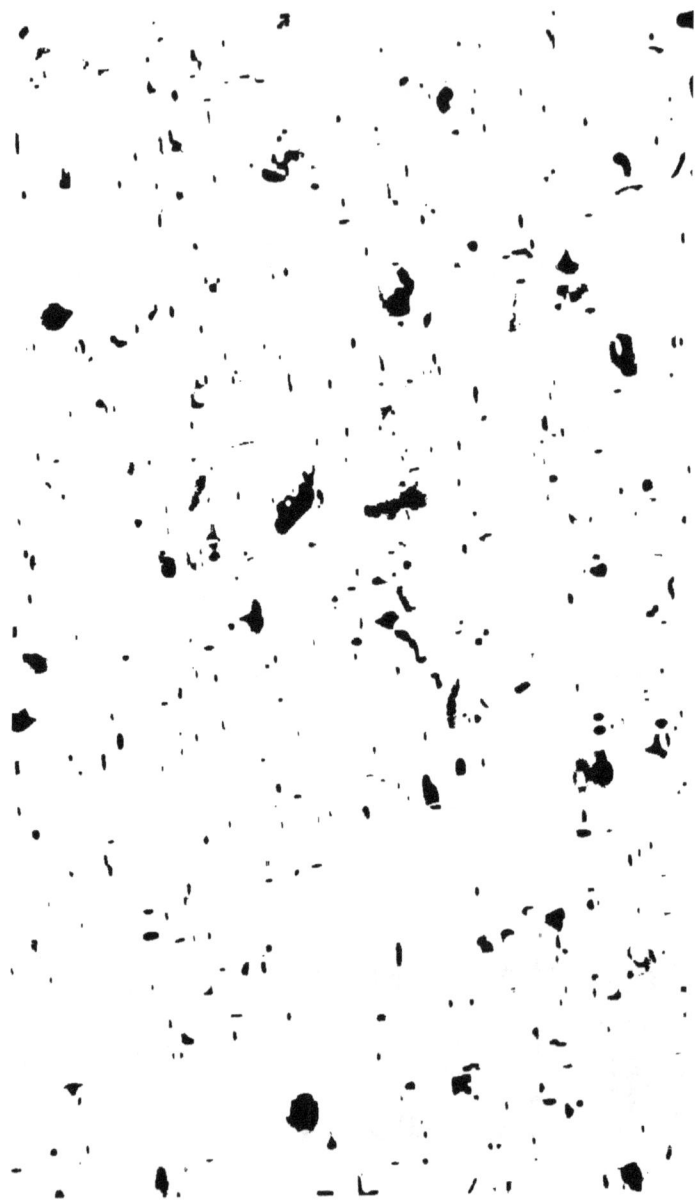

THE

POCUMTUC HOUSEWIFE;

A GUIDE TO

DOMESTIC COOKERY,

AS IT IS PRACTICED IN THE CONNECTICUT VALLEY.

To which are added plain directions for soap-making, brewing, candle dipping, clear starching, caring for the sick and all duties of a careful housewife.

❧

Especially adapted to the use of young wives who come from outside places and are not conversant with the ways of the Valley, and of female orphans who have not had a mother's training.

BY SEVERAL LADIES.

DEERFIELD:
First Edition 1805,
Reprint with additions 1897.

PUBLISHED BY
WILLARD LEND A HAND SOCIETY,
DEERFIELD, MASS.

Contents.

3

Note to the Edition of 1897.

✣

TO THE READER.

IN the universal hunt for things ancestral, one essential part of the old life has been neglected. Why should empty platters and plates be cherished as something sacred, and the contents for which alone they existed be forgotten? Surely, a dish of pudding had a closer connection with a grandfather, than a dish of Canton china. In a sense the pudding was itself an ancestor. The blood it fed still flows in living veins. Then let *it* be honored and its history told!

Does anyone doubt the comparative merit of willow ware cookery and that of the present day? Ask any man or woman of years sufficient to remember the brick oven and the roasting spit, and doubt no longer. Stove cooked food merely sustains life. Some housewives are unfortunately placed in ready made houses without ovens or wide fireplaces. These cannot hope to excel. By carefully following as far as may be the rules found in this little book, they may gain some faint idea of the homemade ambrosia on which the men of old were fed.

4

Advertisement to First Edition.

❧

AS the directions which follow, were intended for the conduct of the families of the authoress's own Daughters, and for the arrangement of their Table, so as to unite a good Figure with proper Economy, she has avoided all excessive luxury, such as essence of Ham, and that wasteful expenditure of large quantities of meat for Gravy, which so greatly contributes to keep up the price, and is no less injurious to those who eat, than to those whose penury bids them abstain. Many receipts are given for things which, being in daily Use, the mode of preparing them may be supposed too well known to require a place in a cookery book; yet how rarely do we meet with fine melted butter, good Toast and water, or well made Coffee! She makes no apology for minuteness in some articles or for leaving others unnamed, because she writes not for professed Cooks. This little work would have been a treasure to herself, when she first set out in life, and she therefore hopes it may be useful to others. In that idea it is given to the public, and as she will receive from it no Emolument, so she trusts it will escape without Censure.

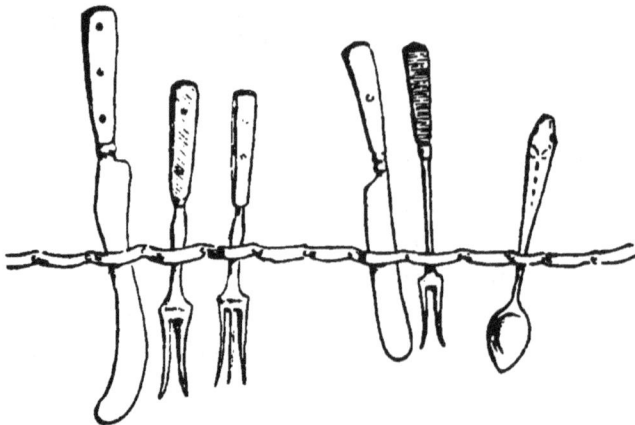

What to Eat.

It will not be out of place to suggest to a Novice what will be expected in the way of Meals in a farmer's household with a good many hands to feed.

For Breakfast.

For Sunday morning in winter fry the hasty-pudding that was left over from Saturday night's supper. Eat it with West India molasses or Muscovado sugar. In summer fried pudding is too heating. Pancakes with Cider and Sugar are better. Flapjacks are good on holidays or when the men folks are not working hard. Week day mornings farmers want some meat that can be cooked quickly, so as to let them go to the meadows before the sun is up. Sausages, Ham, Souse, fried Pork and eggs, or pork and apple with a milk gravy, with Irish potatoes boiled, are always handy. Salt Mackerel and Shad freshened over night and boiled are good. When the Shad catch comes, buy a Barrel of them and salt them yourself. They are very

6

nice. Johnny cake or hoe cakes are a good change from Rye and indian bread. It is always best to keep flour bread in the house, but with a large family of farm hands or apprentices it cannot be eaten commonly. Nut cakes are expected for breakfast and sometimes Pye.

It is a good Rule for young children to eat a Bowl of bread and milk in the morning before coming to the table.

For Dinner.

Some families like to get up a great dinner on Sundays and have friends who drive to Meeting from a distance come in for the Nooning. There is no objection to this if everything is prepared the day before. The meat should be plain Roast so that it can be started and left. A young child can tend the Spit while the rest of the family is away. In winter the Pyes should be put on the hearth before meeting, also, so as to thaw gradually. If you wish to avoid the necessity of keeping anyone at home, get some rice Porridge or brewis and cold meat. This with Pye is enough for anyone on a leisure day. For a week day dinner boiled corned beef and pork with a pudding and seasonable vegetables is a standard dish, and always relished by working men. Lay in a good supply of Turnips and cabbages, Pumpkins and squashes. Calf's head and pluck makes a filling meal. You can have fresh meat frequently, even in warm weather, if when you kill a sheep or calf you pass it around to the neighbors, and they return the Compliment when they kill. It is usually safer to wait for cool Weather before killing beef and pork. Fowls are always to be had. When the team goes to Boston in the winter with a load to sell, have it bring back a fifty pound fresh codfish, and a barrel of oysters along with the molasses and sugar supply. The fish will keep frozen for weeks. A piece can be sawed off and thawed when needed. It can be salted down, and is much better than store codfish.

7

☞Store Codfish is not bad eating if properly cooked, but both it and the people who eat it are held in disrepute. They used to say that the Wisdom men came to the store every Saturday night to get a Codfish for Sunday, until the loafers began to sing:

" Conway for beauty, Deerfield for pride.
If it hadn't been for Codfish, Wisdom would have died."

as soon as a Wisdomite appeared.

For company and great occasions, of course roast pig and turkey and various delicacies will be cooked. These suggestions are for every day.

Supper.

Arrange the cold meat and vegetables left from dinner on a large platter for the men folks. Saturday night they will expect hasty-pudding and milk, or Samp when corn is new. Brown bread and Milk with pumpkin stewed dry, or baked sweet Apples, or huckleberries, are liked on a hot summer afternoon, especially if the milk is hung down the well and cooled. Pie and gingerbread and custards are good enough for common use. Keep a loaf of Rich Cake on hand for unexpected company.

Baking Day.

*

How to Heat the Oven.

Mrs. L. M. Child says, " Economical People will use fagots and brush to heat the Oven." Hard wood heats it quicker and hotter. Take four foot wood split fine and pile it criss-cross so as to nearly fill the Oven, and keep putting in.

☞Some have thought it saved fuel to set fire to the house immediately around the oven. This is doubtful economy and the Oven is apt to be overheated.

8

A roaring Fire for an Hour or more is usually enough. The Top and Sides will at first be covered with black soot. See that it is all burned off. Rake the Coals over the bottom and let them lie a minute. Then sweep it out clean. If you can hold your hand inside while you count Forty it is about right for flour bread; to count twenty is right for Rye and indian.

Bake the Brown bread first, then flour bread and Pies, then Cake or puddings, and last custards. After everything else is out put in a pan of apples. Next morning they will be deliciously baked. A pot of Beans can be baking back side, out of the way, with the Rest.

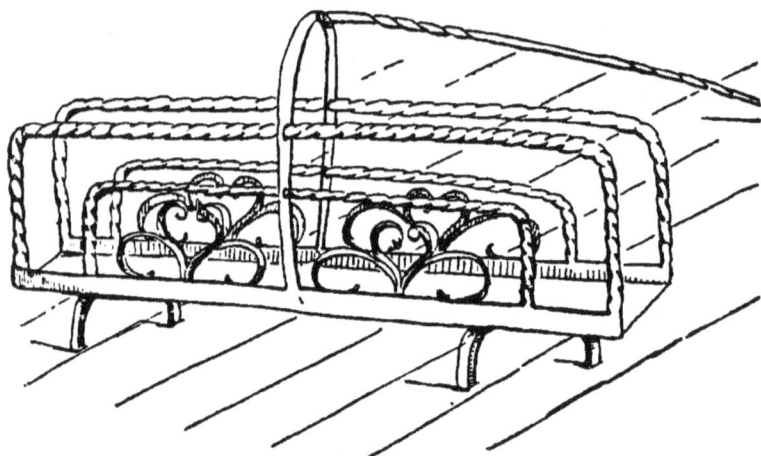

Bread.

❧

Emptins. Nothing raises bread so well as good lively beer Emptins. If it is saved every time the beer keg is emptied you will always have a fresh Supply. Some small families do not brew every week. In that case make a flour thickening, pour on scalding water to make a Batter. Put in a cup of emptins. When it is risen bottle and cork well. This will keep ten days or more. If it spoils borrow some of a neighbor who has fresh.

☞Fleischman, the brewer, makes quite a business of saving his beer emptins, thickening it so as to make it into cakes, and selling these around to people who are not provident enough to supply themselves. It is said to be very good.

Rye and Indian.   Miss Louisa Stebbins.

Put six or eight quarts each of Rye meal and Indian meal, and a little salt into the bread trough and stir them together. Wet with milk and a pint of emptins, making it very stiff. Let it rise over night, mould it into loaves in the morning, and bake on the bottom of the oven. Put it way back with the bread slice so as to be out of the way. The longer it bakes the sweeter it tastes. Stewed Pumpkin stirred in with the milk is good.

Rye Bread is made the same way.

Flour Bread is not made quite so stiff and is baked in pans.

If bread runs short before baking day comes, light cakes can be baked in the bake kettle or the tin baker. Draw out a solid mass of Coals, set the bake kettle over it, put in your biscuit, put on the lid, and cover it with a thick layer of coals.

Raised Biscuit are made much like bread except that a little shortening is used and they are allowed to get lighter. In winter, biscuit dough can be kept on hand a long time. When company comes, cut off a piece, mold it up and bake it.

Rolls (like Sally Lumm's). By a Lady, Phil. 1808.

Warm one ounce of butter in half a pint of milk. Put to it a spoonful and a half of yeast of small beer, and a little salt. Put two pounds of flour into a pan and mix in the above. Let it rise an hour. Knead it well. Make into seven rolls and bake in a quick oven. If made in cakes three inches thick, sliced and buttered, they resemble Sally Lumm's as made at Bath.

Muffins.   Mrs. M. S. Allen.

One quart of milk, one-half cup yeast, two eggs, tablespoon butter, little salt. Flour to mix very thick. Let it rise over night. In the morning stir in a little soda and bake half an hour.

Rusk.

Make a batter of one pint warm milk, one-half cup yeast and flour, one teaspoon salt and let it rise over night. In the morning add one-half teacup butter, two well beaten eggs and flour enough to roll. Cut into round cakes. Put one on another to bake, let them stand half an hour, then bake. When done split open, pile lightly in a pan and dry in a slow oven till crisp.

Sally Lunn. MRS. LAURA WELLS

One quart flour, butter size of an egg, three tablespoons sugar, two eggs, two teacups milk, two teaspoons cream tartar, one teaspoon soda, salt. Bake in a large pan and break up.

Brown Bread, (Sweetened) MRS. F. STEBBINS

Two cups Indian meal, four cups rye meal, one cup molasses, salt, one cup raisins, one teaspoon soda. Mix with buttermilk or sour milk, soft.

Brown Bread.

Two cups Indian meal, two cups rye, one cup flour, one and one-half pints sweet milk, one teaspoon soda, one tablespoon vinegar added last. Steam three hours, or boil. Remove lid and brown in oven ten minutes.

Johnny Cake.

One pint buttermilk, one pint meal, one pint flour, one egg, one heaping teaspoon soda, one tablespoon sugar, salt.

A Hoe Cake is made of Indian meal and water and a
little salt, mixed very stiff and baked on a plate or a clean board before a very hot fire.

Fire Cakes. MISS LOUISA STEBBINS.

Make a dough like pie crust of flour, lard, salt, and water, only use less lard. Roll out thin and cover plates with it, pinching the edges to make it stick. Put a row of flat irons around a brisk fire and set the plates against them.—When they are brown one side, slip and turn them and brown the other.

Aunt Mary's Pancakes.   MRS. C. H. ASHLEY.

One quart buttermilk, one teaspoon soda, one egg, salt.
Mix rather stiff. Drop from a spoon into hot fat and fry brown.
To be eaten with sugar and cider.

Indian Flapjacks.

Scald a quart of Indian meal. When lukewarm stir in half
a pint of flour, half a teacup of yeast, salt. When light fry.

Flour Flapjacks.

Make a batter of buttermilk, flour, pearlash and salt, just
thick enough to spread easily. Put enough in a long handled
frying pan to cover the bottom. When one side is done just
right, give the pan a little jerk to loosen the cake, then toss it
up with bit of a twist, and catch it fairly when it comes down
the other side up. Pile the cakes on a platter as fast as they
cook, spreading each with butter and sugar, and, on extra occasions, a little nutmeg grated over. Cut the pile down through
in sections like a pie, in serving.

☞Every family has a legend of an inexpert but muscular fryer of flapjacks, who tossed so high, the cakes flapped up through the wide kitchen
chimney and came down outside. This should be avoided.

RHODE ISLAND CAKES.   MRS. YALE.

Stir together meal, salt and a little butter. Pour on boiling
water to make a thick batter. Drop into a hot spider in which
salt pork has just been fried Set it back where it will brown
crisply without burning. Fry about an hour for both sides. The
cakes should be an inch thick, light and tender.

Meats.

✤

Grandmother Arms' Boiled Dinner.

If it was to be a boiled dinner grandmother and one of the
girls would set about it as soon as breakfast was well out of the
way.   First they made sure the fire was good and steady, such
a one as would last till dinner was served.   Then the great dinner pot was hung on the crane and fillled half full of cold water.
Into this was plumped a big piece of corned beef and another
of fat pork.

At nine o'clock grandmother would lift the cover and if the
kettle was boiling would place the pudding pot beside the beef
and pork.   At the same time Polly would bring the beets and
go back to the work of scraping, peeling and washing the other
vegetables.

At half past ten the cabbage went in, at eleven the carrots
and turnips, at half past eleven parsnips and potatoes.   Then

quarters of squash were laid on the top and the dinner was under way.

The great square table was next pulled out, covered with a plain home-spun cloth and the pewter plates and mugs, the steel knives and two-tined forks laid for ten people. At the corners were placed huge plates of "rye and injun" bread, pats of butter, also pickled cucumbers, cabbage or mangoes and pitchers filled with cider and beer.

In Deerfield the conch shell and the dinner horn were unnecessary for as the sun reached high noon the old sexton rang a general invitation to stop work and go home to dinner from the belfry of the old church. At this signal the great pewter platter would be placed in the center of the table. The beef and pork half hidden in the substantial garnish of crimson beets, white potatoes, thick moist slices of pinkish turnip, golden carrots and yellow parsnips, with here and there squash and cabbage. The last thing on the table was the huge, smoking, red-brown Indian Pudding and when the clattering of chairs had subsided and the board was surrounded by hungry men fresh from the beautifying influence of bar soap and rough crash, hungry children fresh from intellectual inspiration of birch and book, hungry cooks and helpers, it was to the pudding they were first served, each receiving a generous slice to be eaten with butter and "West Injer" molasses. Then grandfather carved the meat and everybody helped himself, pouring on plenty of cider vinegar and home-made mustard to stimulate digestion. One might suppose the following day would be an easy one for these busy women, and a vision of a cold dinner in a cool kitchen begin to rise. Let us not deceive ourselves, that dinner was for that day and if by reason of quantity some yet remained after the meal was ended, it was put on cold for suppper with the pie and doughnuts and custards. The next day dinner began anew.

Roasts of beef, mutton, lamb and veal were not so uncommon as many would have us believe, while many chickens and turkeys failed to grace the Thanksgiving board from having been cut off at a tender age to assist at some family jollification.

Fricasseed Chicken.   MISS. ELIZA WILLIAMS.

Joint the chicken and boil gently till tender. When done fry slices of salt pork to a delicate brown, take from the fry-pan and arrange on platter. Put the chicken, which has meantime been draining, into the pan and brown in the pork fat.

Thicken the chicken broth with flour mixed smooth with water, add some butter the last thing, pour part of this gravy over the chicken which has been placed on the platter with the pork around it. The rest of the gravy should be poured over toast in another dish.

Fried Cod Fish.

Soak cod fish over night in cold water. Cut in pieces about two inches square, roll in Indian meal and fry with salt pork.

Pork and Apple.

Fry slices of pork until crisp and dry, take out of the frying pan and pour off a part of the fat. Take some large fair apples cut in round slices leaving the skin on; place these in the remainder of the fat and salt and when done serve like fritters. Apple is also good fried with sausage.

Pork and Cream.   MRS. YALE.

Fry slices of salt pork to a delicate brown. Take out into a deep dish. Turn part of the fat out of the frying pan and pour in thick cream, as soon as it is hot pour it over the pork.

Pork Fried in Batter.

Dip slices of freshly fried pork into a plain batter and fry like griddle cakes.

Cracker Hash. MRS. JENKS.

Chop cold roast meat fine. Add gravy and water to make very moist, butter size of an egg, salt, pepper and sage; heat through and cover with a thick layer of cracker crumbs. Bake one hour.

Vegetable Hash. MRS. APOLLOS ROOT.

Take whatever remains of the meat, beets, carrots, turnips, and potatoes, after a boiled dinner, chop fine, pour into a pan in which a bit of pork has been fried, cover and brown.

Calf's Head and Pluck. MISS L. STEBBINS.

Soak the head in ashes and water, scald and scrape. It must be cleaned with great care. The head, heart and lights should be boiled full two hours. One hour is enough for the pluck. The brains should be thoroughly washed and put in a bag with a pounded cracker and a litttle sifted sage and boiled one hour then broken up with a knife, peppered, salted and buttered, and put in a bowl by themselves. Make a sauce of butter and flour and boiling water and serve with the head.

Sea Pie.

This pie is so called because it was brought to Western New England long ago by a sea captain. In order to make it you first take a piece of pork or veal, or anything you happen to have. Put it "a bilin" in the great iron pot over the fire, add a quart of sweet dried apples, some salt if necessary and "bile" till the meat is nearly done. Then add a cup of molasses and dumplings of the ordinary pot pie description.

☞Strange as it may seem to modern taste this compound of dissimilar materials was much prized. It was the favorite dish of "Uncle Oliver" Smith.

During the last year of Uncle Oliver's life he was in miserable health. It became necessary for him to make a trip to Boston on businesss (a serious undertaking in those days). He said that he felt too weak to go but a sea-pie, he thought, might set him up and enable him to accomplish his mission. So "Aunt Lois" who "looked after him" bestirred herself and succeeded in finding some dried sweet apples, (sea pies were then going out of fashion) made a pie and set it before him. Having partaken of which he was so strengthened that he made the journey and settled his business.

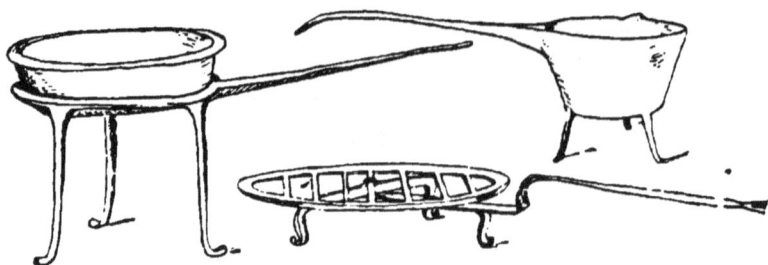

Directions for Roasting.

❧

If the thing to be roasted be thin and tender the fire should be little and brisk. When you have a large joint to roast make up a sound strong fire, equally good in every part. Let it be proportioned to the dinner to be dressed and about three or four inches longer at each end than the thing to be roasted.

Pins and skewers can by no means be allowed they are so many taps to let out the gravy.

The first preparation for roasting is to take care that the spit be properly cleaned with sand and water, nothing else.

Never salt your roast meat before you lay it down to the fire, (except ribs) for that will draw out the gravy.

To Roast Beef.

Wash it, spit it and lay it before the fire from one and a half to two hours according to the size of the roast.

To Roast a Pig.   "ECONOMICAL HOUSEKEEPER."

Prepare some stuffing as for a turkey, fill it full and sew it up with a coarse thread; flour it well over and keep flouring till the eyes drop out, or you find the crackling hard. Be sure to save all the gravy that comes out of it by setting basins or pans under the pig in the dripping-pan, as soon as the gravy begins to run. When the pig is done enough stir the fire up; take a coarse cloth with a piece of butter in it, and rub the pig over till the crackling is crisp; then take it up. Lay it in a dish, and with a sharp knife cut off the head, then cut the pig in two be_ fore you draw out the spit. Cut the ears off the head, and lay them at each end; cut the under jaw in two and lay the parts at each side; melt some good butter, take the gravy you saved and put in it, boil it, pour it in the dish with the brains bruised fine and some sage mixed together, and then send it to the table. If just killed, a pig will require an hour to roast; if killed the day before, an hour and a quarter, if a very large one, an hour and a half.

Roast Turkey.

Wash the turkey carefully inside and out, fill the crop and then the body with your stuffing, sew it up, hang by a stout cord from the hook in the ceiling before a steady fire. Keep it turn- ing till done. Serve with cranberry or turnip sauce.

To Broil Shad, Mackerel or Salmon.

Have the bars of the gridiron well greased with lard lay your fish on, flesh side down; when half done turn it and finish. When done pour over sweet cream if you have it, or spread over a little butter.

Chicken Pie.   Mrs. Frank Nims.

Boil the chickens. Take out all the bones except the drum- sticks, second joints and wings.

Line a milk pan with paste, put in the meat, sweeten and season to taste. Cut a large hole in the top crust before cover- ing the pie.

Two quarts of flour are sufficient for the paste, stir with it six teaspoons of baking powder, and add three cups of shorten- ing. Mix as for pie crust, and wet with milk to make a soft dough.

19

Baked Beans.

For an ordinary sized family put a quart of beans to soak at night. In the morning set them on the stove till they come to a boil then pour off the water. Add more cold water and half a pound of salt pork with the rind scored, let it come to a boil, season with a tablespoon of molasses and one of sugar, as much salt as necessary (the pork will not salt it quite enough) put it into pan or crock and bake all day in a slow oven. If the water dries out before the beans are done add more. If the oven is hotter than need be the dish should be covered at first. The cranberry bean is more desirable than any other kind for this purpose.

Directions for Pickling and Preserving Meats.

✤

Corned Beef.

For a hundred pounds of beef take seven pounds of salt, four pounds of brown sugar and four ounces of salt petre; mix together. Place a layer of the mixture at the bottom of the barrel, then a layer of beef and so on. A heavy weight should be placed on top.

Pickled Pig's Feet.

Scrape and wash the pig's feet, cover with salt and water; let stand two days then put in more salt and let stand two days more; boil about two hours, slip out the bones and pour vinegar over them, with a few cloves and a stick of cinnamon.

Sausage.   MRS. CHAS. JONES, Little Mary Hawks.

Chop fresh pork fine. For twenty pounds of meat use seven ounces of salt, three ounces of sage, one and a half ounces of pepper. Put in bags or skins. Fry or bake.

To Pickle Ham.

To a hundred weight put eight pounds salt, six pounds sugar, four ounces salt petre, two ounces of saleratus and water enough to cover.

Souse.   MRS. M. S. STEBBINS.

Pigs feet, ears, skins, etc., should be scalded and cleaned. Boil four or five hours, until very soft, Skim out and pack in a jar, throwing in cloves, salt, pepper, as it is put in. Put a plate and a weight on top. Pour over hot vinegar. Cut in slices, dip in flour, and fry brown.

Head Cheese.

Boil head and cheeks until the meat drops from the bones. Chop fine, season high with salt, pepper, sage, (summer savory if you like). Put in a colander or cheese press, cover and put weights on top to drain it. When cold serve.

Pies.

*

At some seasons of the year, fresh pie timber runs short. Make a good deal of rich mince meat in the fall. With occasional scalding it may be kept nearly the year round. A bushel of dried apples helps fill the gap. Carrot, grated and cooked like squash, makes delicious pies. A pie of boiled raisins chopped, with a rolled cracker stirred in, require very little extra seasoning and is not expensive. If all things fail, puddings must be substituted, but they do not take the place.

At Thanksgiving time, it saves labor to make seventy-five or a hundred pies, and keep them on hand. Freeze them and slip the covered ones from the plates. Pack them in an earthen crock, or a large chest, one upon another.

Pie Crust.

One quart of pastry flour, one cup of lard, salt. Mix with a knife and wet with cold water until you can roll it. Fold over and roll again into shape.

Cranberry Pie.

Fill a covered plate with uncooked cranberries, add half a cup of molasses and four tablespoons of sugar. Cover with an upper crust, and bake half an hour in a quick oven.

22

Marborough Pie.

Steam until tender six large tart apples, and strain. Stir in one spoonful butter; when cool, add two eggs, the rind and juice of a lemon, and one cup of sugar beaten together. Bake with one crust.

Pumpkin Pie.

One quart sifted pumpkin, one pint milk, two eggs, one cup sugar, salt, nutmeg, and a little ginger. Bake with one crust.

Pumpkin Pie Without Eggs.

One quart pumpkin, five tablespoons flour, two quarts milk. Sweeten to taste with molasses and sugar; season with ginger, allspice, cinnamon, and a pinch of cloves. Place over boiling water, and stir until it thickens. Bake with one crust.

Raisin Pie.

One cup seeded raisins, one half cup sugar, one tablespoon ginger, salt and spice. Boil the raisins in a cup of water; add a spoonful of flour and one egg. Bake in two crusts.

Mince Pie. Miss Avis Arms.

One third each of meat, suet and apple chopped fine, also citron and raisins. Moisten with molasses and cider, or sweet pickle vinegar; add one cup sugar, salt, nutmeg, clove and cinnamon, lemon rind, if liked.

Rhubarb or Persian Apple. Mrs. Luke Wright.

One cup chopped rhubarb, one cup sugar, one egg, one table-spoon flour, one-third rind of lemon grated.

Cream Pie. Mrs. J. Stebbins.

One cup cream, one egg, one cup maple sugar, one table-spoon flour, small piece of butter.

Squash Pie.

MRS. F. STEBBINS.

One cup sifted squash, one egg, one half cup sugar, one table-spoon flour, one pint milk, one half cup raisins seeded and spread on the pastry, salt and cinnamon.

Lemon Pie.

Juice and grated rind of one lemon, one cup of sugar, one cup water, two tablespoons flour, salt. Flour and water boiled together; white of egg partly reserved for frosting with a spoonful of sugar.

Sweet Potato Pie.

Slice boiled potatoes into a covered plate; add sugar, a sprinkle of flour, salt; then another layer of potatoes, more sugar, a bit of butter, nutmeg. Pour in milk and bake slowly.

Cheese Cakes.

MRS. JENKS.

Two cups soft cottage cheese, two eggs beaten light, one cup sugar, butter size of a walnut, nutmeg and cinnamon. Pour in a crust and bake a rich brown.

Marborough Puddings.

MRS. BAKER.

One pint strained stewed apple, three-fourths pound butter, one pound sugar. Mix while warm; when cool, add five eggs well beaten, nutmeg and cinnamon, one half cup cream. Bake with one crust; makes four pies.

Apple Pudding Pie.

Five cups strained stewed apple; add while hot a small cup of butter, two cups of sugar, and beat thoroughly. Then add five eggs beaten light, two and a half cups of rich milk, spice to taste.

24

Fried Pies.

One cup buttermilk, one egg, salt, half teaspoon soda, flour to roll; divide in four parts. Roll in a thin sheet as large as can be fried in the kettle, turn, and when done, spread with hot apple sweetened, and a dust of cinnamon; or roll doughnut dough thin, cut in pieces, lay on a spoonful of apple sauce, wet and pinch together the edges like a turnover and fry in boiling lard.

Pan Pies.   Mrs. Ingersoll.

Pare, core and quarter half a peck of apples and fill a very deep earthen pan. Add one cup of water and one cup of brown sugar. Cover with a thick crust of risen bread dough into which you have worked a large tablespoonful of butter. Let rise a short time. Bake in a brick oven, after the first heat is gone, all night. In the morning, while the pie is still warm, take off the crust, cut in slices and put in the bottom of two large pudding dishes. Season the apple to taste with molasses, allspice and cinnamon, a teaspoonful of each spice, pour over the crust, cover with a plate and return to the oven for half an hour to become thoroughly softened. This served for breakfast or lunch was considered most delectable by the children of by-gone days.

Pan Dowdy.   Miss Judith Allen.

Cover a deep pie plate with crust. Put in a layer of sliced apple, then thin shavings of salt pork, then more apple and more pork. Bake with an upper crust. When done cake off the crust, season the apple with sugar, molasses, allspice or what you choose. Put half the apple in upper crust turned over like a plate, lay on the rest of the apple and serve hot.

Stebbins Pudding.

One pound bread, one quart milk; soak over night. In the morning sift through a colander, add seven eggs, three-fourths pound of butter, nutmeg and raisins, aud another half pint of milk.

Apple Dumplings.

Make a good biscuit crust; peel and core tart apples; fill with sugar; wrap each in a piece of dough.

Steam or bake one hour.

Serve with butter and sugar sauce.

Puddings.

Boiled Indian Pudding.

Sifted Indian meal and warm milk (not scalding or pudding will break to pieces) should be stirred together stiff. A little salt, and two or three great spoonfuls of molasses; a spoonful of ginger. Boil it in a tight covered pan, or a very thick cloth. Leave plenty of room for Indian swells very much. Some people chop sweet suet fine and warm in the milk; others warm thin slices of sweet apple to be stirred into the pudding. Water will answer instead of milk. Boil four or five hours.

A Tasty Pudding.

One quart milk, scald and stir in one cup meal, one cup molasses, two large spoons cider molasses, a little salt, and butter, a little sour apple sliced thin. Bake slowly for three hours.

Baked Indian Pudding.   Miss Whiting.

One quart milk, five table spoons of meal, three fourths cup of molasses, salt, cinnamon. Scald a pint of milk, stir in the meal. When cool, add the egg. Bake slowly for two hours, adding the rest of the milk while baking.

Apple Slump.   Mrs. E. Cowles.

Fill small stew pan one-third full of quartered apple; add one cup sugar, two thirds cup molasses, nutmeg, cloves and cinnamon; cover and cook a very little. Make a biscuit dough without shortening, roll one inch thick and cover the apple. Cook slowly for an hour, covered; then let it brown. Lift the crust, break in pieces and pour apple over. The quarters should be whole and clear.

Baked Rice Pudding.   Miss E. Williams.

One teacup rice, two and a half quarts of milk, one half teaspoon salt, a small cup of sugar, half a cup of raisins, cinnamon and nutmeg. Put part of the milk to the rice and set on the stove to cook, adding the rest of the milk, hot as it is needed. Cook slowly, stirring often for about two hours. Then bake in a moderate oven one hour.

Rice Pudding with Eggs.

Two cups boiled rice, one quart of milk, three eggs, a teaspoonful of salt, small piece of butter, nutmeg or lemon to taste. Bake thirty-five minutes.

Sweet Corn Pudding.   Miss E. Williams.

Take twelve ears of corn, cut the rows through the center and scrape out the pulp with a knife. Add three eggs, a pint of milk, and a spoonful of butter. Sweeten and flavor to taste. Bake one half hour.

Plum Pudding.

MRS. JENKS.

Half a loaf of bread in crumbs, pour over a quart of cold milk. Let stand several hours, then mash fine. Add seven eggs, a cup of sugar, one fourth cup of butter, spice and a pint of raisins. Bake three or four hours.

Pudding Sauce.

One cup sugar, two tablespoons butter, one large tablespoonful of flour, stirred together. Add one beaten egg, salt, a gill of boiling water, tablespoonful of vinegar and teaspoon of vanilla, or wine if preferred.

English Plum Pudding.

A stale loaf of baker's bread grated, ten eggs, half a pound of sugar, one pound suet, one cup molasses, one and one half pounds stoned raisins, one pound currants, two ounces citron, one teaspoon each of cloves, cinnamon and nutmeg, one glass of brandy and one of wine. Boil in a cloth six hours or steam in a mould. Serve with sweet sauce.

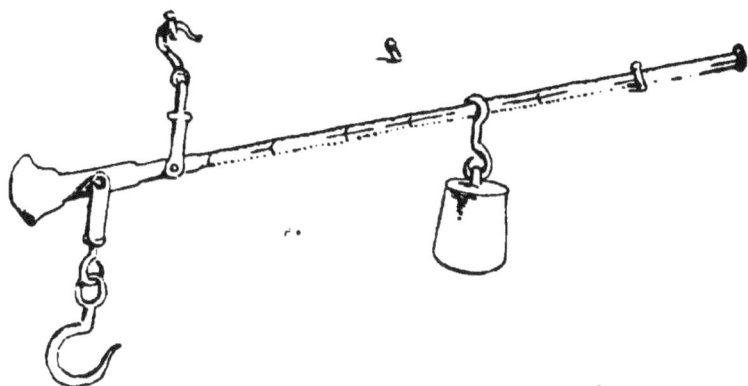

Cake.

&

The production of good cake requires particular care and every careful housewife will take pains to perfect herself in this necessary art. Every well-regulated family will keep a sufficient quantity of rich fruit cake on hand for chance visitors or other occasions. This can be made before Thanksgiving, of a richness to ensure its keeping six or even twelve months. Should it become mouldy on the outside the mould can be removed with a damp cloth and the cake set into a hot oven for a few moments when it will become as good as new.

Gingerbread, seedcakes and doughnuts will suffice for daily needs. In all cases where spices are named it is supposed they be pounded fine and sifted, sugar must be dried and rolled fine, flour dried in an oven, eggs well beat or whipped to a raging foam. Pearlash is a necessary ingredient in all cakes made with sour or butter-milk. Thrifty housekeepers are wont to gather the whitest and lightest of applewood ashes as they fall in the fireplace. These should be leached with water and put into bottles.

A manufactured article called soda is used in conjunction with cream tartar and sweet milk to make light delicious cakes.

Wedding Cake.   MRS. CATHARINE HOYT.

Three pounds of raisins, two pounds of currants, one half pound citron, a pound of flour, same of butter and sugar; one tablespoon mace or nutmeg, one ounce of cinnamon and one of cloves, a little molasses, a wine glass of wine, eleven eggs, Stir sugar and butter to a cream then add eggs beaten separately, next flour then the other things.

Honeymoon Cake.

Three fourths of a cup of butter, one and a fourth cups sugar, one-half cup of milk, two eggs, spice, one teaspoon cream tartar, one half teaspoon soda, two and a half cups flour.

Six Months Cake.   MRS. FRANK STEBBINS.

Two cups sugar, one and a half cups butter, four eggs, one cup molasses, one cup sweet milk, spices to taste, two cups raisins, one cup citron, one cup currants, one teaspoon saleratus, four and a half cups flour.

Election Cake.

Four pounds flour, two and a half pounds sugar, two pounds butter, one scant quart of milk, eight eggs, one half pint wine two nutmegs, two teaspoonfuls of cinnamon, one teaspoon of cloves, two gills yeast. Make up flour, yeast and milk exactly like bread; when light add other ingredients. When again light add one pound of currants, two pounds of raisins. Bake two hours.

Raised Cake.   MRS. SAMUEL WELLS.

One and a half cups of bread dough, one cup of sugar, one half cup of butter, one egg, a little soda, nutmeg and cinnamon to taste, a cup full of chopped raisins.

Bake as soon as made.

Pound Cake.

A pound of butter and the same of sugar and flour, ten eggs, two pounds raisins, one pound currants, half a pound of citron one teaspoon soda, spices if one likes.

One Two Three Four Cake.

A cup of butter, two of sugar, three of flour, four eggs. Beat well together and bake in cups or pans for twenty minutes.

Hoosac Loaf Cake.

One and three fourths pounds of flour and the same of sugar, three fourths of a pound of butter, three fourths of a pound of raisins, a pint of milk, four eggs, a glass of wine, one nutmeg, a teaspoon of soda.

Aunt Emily's Cake.

A cup of butter, two cups of sugar, one cup of milk, four cups of flour, three eggs, a teaspoon of soda, two teaspoons cream tarter, extract lemon, a little nutmeg, a dash of brandy, one cup of raisins and a cup of citron sliced fine. Bake fifty-five minutes.

Little Plum Cakes to Keep Long.   1805.

A coffee cup of sugar, a cup of butter, a little less than a quart of flour. Beat the butter to a cream, add three eggs well beaten, a quarter of a pound of currants, the same of citron, the sugar and flour, and a little brandy. Beat all for some time then dredge flour on tin plates and drop the batter on them the size of a walnut. Bake in a brisk oven.

Sponge Cake.

Ten eggs, the weight of the eggs in sugar, the weight of five eggs in flour, grated peel and juice of a lemon. Beat the yolks and sugar together till white and creamy, whip the whites to a stiff froth, put together and stir in flour lightly, adding lemon last. This receipt has been used for several generations in one family and is much prized.

Shrewsbury Cakes.

A pound of butter, three fourths pound of sugar, a little mace, four eggs. Mix and beat with your hand till very light. Put this composition to a pound of flour. Roll it into small cakes. Bake with a light oven.

Blueberry Cake.

A scant cup of sugar, an egg, a pinch of salt, a cup of milk, two teaspoons baking powder, one and a half cups of berries, flour to make a thick batter. Bake in cups or small tins.

Mollie Saunder's Upper Shelf Gingerbread.

Three and a half pounds of flour, a pound of butter, a quart of Sugar-house molasses boiled with the butter, a tablespoon of soda dissolved in warm water, ginger to your taste. Roll it on flat tin sheets and print with corrugated squares made for the purpose. Mollie Saunder's Lower Shelf Gingerbread had no butter in it. These receipts were made by the woman who kept the best bakeshop in Salem about a hundred years ago.

Sugar Gingerbread.

A cup of butter, three cups of sugar, two eggs, a half cup of buttermilk, half a cup of cream, a large teaspoon of soda, two tablespoons of ginger. Some salt and flour to mix very stiff. Roll thin, mark with creased roller and cut in squares.

Great Grandmother's Gingerbread.

Four pounds of flour, two pounds of sugar, a pound and a half of butter, a teaspoon of soda dissolved in tablespoonful

32

rose water or milk, eight eggs, a half teacup of ginger. Roll very thin on flat tin sheets. This is a very old recipe but still in use.

Cream Gingerbread.

One cup molasses, one egg, one half cup cream, one and a half cups of flour, a teaspoon of soda, ginger and salt to taste.

Soft Gingerbread.

One cup molasses, one heaping teaspoon ginger, one teaspoon full soda, a little salt, a heaping tablespoon butter, two thirds of a cup of boiling water, two cups of flour.

Buttermilk Gingerbread.

One and a half cups of molasses, one half a cup of sugar, a cup and a half of buttermilk, a third of a cup of shortening, a little salt, cinnamon and ginger to taste, a teaspoon of soda. Flour to make stiff.

Ginger Snaps.

Two cups of molasses, a cup of sugar, one of butter, three teaspoons of ginger and two of soda. Roll very thin and bake in a quick oven.

Cream Cookies.

A cup of sugar, a cup of thick cream, a level teaspoon of salt, a rounding teaspooon of soda, two and three fourths cups of flour.

Caraway Cookies.   MRS. WHITING.

One and a half cups of sugar, one cup of butter, one cup of milk, one egg, caraway seeds to taste and flour enough to work. Roll about a quarter of an inch thick.

Crullers, Matrimony or Love Knots.

Three eggs, a cup of sugar, a tablespoon melted butter, one fourth teaspoon soda, nutmeg, flour to make very stiff. Roll thin, cut in strips and tie in knots, or braid three strips together. Fry delicately and sprinkle sugar over while hot.

Doughnuts. MRS. ARMS.

Two eggs, a cup of sugar, a little nutmeg and salt, a tablespoon melted butter, three small teaspoons baking powder, cup and a half of milk, flour to roll. Let them stand before frying.

Rye Doughnuts. MISS JUDITH ALLEN.

Two quarts of rye flour, two thirds of a cup of lard, a pint of milk, a pinch of soda and a level tablespoonful of salt. Mix very hard. Roll one third inch thick in rounds as large as a saucer, cut in strips like a gridiron and twist each strip. Fry fast and crisp.

Raised Doughnuts.

One cupful of lard or butter, two cups of milk, one cup of yeast, three cups of sugar, four or five eggs, nutmeg and a pinch of salt. Warm together the milk and lard, then add the yeast; stir in flour enough to make a batter, and let it stand over night; then add the other ingredients. Knead soft and let rise again; then roll, cut out and let rise before frying.

Custards and Syllabubs.

*

Custard. MRS. BALL.

One and one half pints milk, the same of cream, one cup sugar, seven eggs, a little salt, nutmeg on top.

Raspberry Cream. American Cookery, 1808.

Take a quart of thick sweet cream and boil it two or three wallops. Then take it off the fire and strain the juices of raspberries into it to your taste. Stir it a good while before you put your juice in, that it may be almost cold, and afterwards stir it one way for almost a quarter of an hour. Then sweeten it to your taste and when it is cold you can send it up.

To make a fine Syllabub from the Cow.
American Cookery, 1808.

Sweeten a quart of cider with double refined sugar. Grate nutmeg into it. Then milk your cow into your liquor. When you have thus added what quantity of milk you think proper, pour half a pint or more of the sweetest cream you can get all over it.

Whipped Cream. "American Cookery." 1808.

Take a quart of cream and whites of eight eggs beaten with half a pint of wine; mix them and sweeten to taste with double refined sugar; you may perfume it if you please, with musk or amber gum tied in a rag and steeped a little in the cream. Whip it up with a whisk, with a bit of lemon peel tied to the middle. Take off the froth with a spoon and put it into glasses.

Calf's Foot Jelly.

Scrape four feet clean. Boil in a gallon of water till it is reduced to a quart. Strain and cool. Take off the fat.

Boiled with an equal quantity of milk it makes a good blanc-mange. To make jelly add wine, sugar, juice of lemons, whites of several eggs. Boil and strain into glasses.

35

Porridges and Mushes.

☙

☞ Porridges are always good for children. They make an easy dinner for the women when the men folks take their dinners to the field; and a hot dish of hulled corn and milk or rice porridge is relished by the men on a cold night for supper.

Rag Toast.

Brown all the broken bits of bread in the oven and put them in the bottom of a large dish. Make an ordinary milk porridge and pour over it.

Mulled Buttermilk. MRS. WHITING.

Put buttermilk fresh from the churn to heat with a little salt and sugar. Crumb in a few slices of bread. Let it boil up once and serve.

Hulled Corn. MISS LOUSIA STEBBINS.

Put three or four quarts of old corn in a kettle of water. Tie a handful of ashes in a cloth and put in. Keep the pot warm, but not hot for two or three days. Then pour off the lye and wash the corn thoroughly in many waters, rubbing it together with the hands to loosen the hulls. Let it soak in clear water until you are sure the lye is out. Then boil it slowly for four or five hours, or until it is soft.

Samp.

As soon as the new corn is hard enough not to crush in the mill, have some cracked very coarse. Put as much as you wish for dinner in a pail and pour on cold water. The hulls will rise. Pour off the water carefully through a sieve into a pail, and throw away the chaff. Pour the water back on the corn and stir it up. More hulls will come to the top. Repeat the process until the samp is clean and free from chaff. Boil it like hasty pudding, but longer, using the water you have poured on it to boil it in.

Preserves, Cider Apple Sauce and Pickles.

❧

Mrs. Lydia Maria Child says: "Economical people will seldom use preserves except for sickness. They are unhealthy, expensive and useless to those who are well."

Barberries preserved in molasses are very good for common use. Boil the molasses, skim it, throw in the barberries, and simmer them until they are soft.

A pound of sugar to a pound of fruit is the rule for all preserves. The sugar should be melted over a moderate fire, skimmed clean and the fruit dropped in to simmer until it is soft. Put them in jars, lay a white paper thoroughly wet with brandy flat on the surface of the preserves, and cover tight from the air.

Raspberry Jam.

Six pounds of sugar to ten pounds of berries. Crush the berries and set them over the stove where they will heat slowly. Press through a strainer. Return the juice to the fire and boil briskly fifteen minutes; add the sugar and cook half an hour longer. Put in the fruit and simmer for ten minutes.

Citron Melon Preserves.

Pare and cut the melon in small pieces. Boil gently until tender in just water enough to cover. Skim out and add as much sugar as there was melon. Boil an hour, add the melon and one ·lemon sliced to each pound of melon. Simmer until clear, then take out the melon and lemon and boil the syrup half an hour longer. Pour hot over the melon.

Qnince and Apple Preserve. Mrs. C. E. Williams.

Five pounds quinces pared and quartered, five pounds sweet apples, five pounds sugar. Boil the quince parings and cores in sufficient water to cover. Strain, put in the quince and cook until tender. Take them out and add sugar to water. Let it boil up, then put in quince and apple in alternate layers and cook until apple is tender and red like the quince. Add more water if necessary.

Cider Apple Sauce.

A barrel of cider apple sauce and a half barrel of quince and apple will be needed in an ordinary family. Boil down a barrel of sweet cider as soon as it comes from the press, either in the set kettle or in brass kettles, to ten or twelve gallons. Take a rainy day when the boys are idle to pare the apples. Fill a brass kettle two thirds full with half sweet and half sour quartered apples. Put in two or three quarts of cider syrup and boil until apples are tender. Set the barrel of sauce where it will freeze and it will grow better until spring. It needs time to mature. Sweet apples alone put in a few at a time and skimmed out before they mush are very nice.

The quinces must be sliced very thin and cooked a little before the apple is mixed in.

Save some of the syrup and in the spring make sauce with dried sweet apples first soaked in water.

Syrup for all sorts of Sweet Pickles.

To eight pounds fruit use one quart vinegar, four pounds sugar, one ounce cinnamon stick, one half ounce cloves. Boil together. Put in fruit and skim out when tender. Boil down syrup and pour over fruit.

Preserved Orange Peel.

Sprinkle the peel well with salt and cover with cold water for three or four days. Pour off the brine and put into fresh water to boil until soft; then put into a thick syrup of sugar and water and boil until it is clear. Put it away in jars with the syrup and use it in cakes and puddings as you would citron.

Mangoes.

Take green muskmelons, remove the seeds and put them in salt and water over night. Fill them with onions, horseradish chopped fine, mustard seed and cloves, sew them up and pour over hot vinegar.

Pickled Cabbage.

Pack red cabbages, the large heads cut in quarters, into a brass kettle. Pour weak vinegar and salt over them. Scald until the cabbage is tender. Drain and stick cloves into every piece so as to pin down the leaves. Pack the cabbages in a keg or jar and pour boiling strong vinegar over them.

Tomato Soy.

One peck green tomatoes, six peppers, four onions chopped; add one cup salt and let stand over night. Then drain off the liquid and add a large cup of sugar, a cup of grated horseradish, a tablespoonful each of allspice, cloves and cassia; cover with good vinegar and cook till soft, also add a little ground mustard.

Ripe Tomato Pickle.

Eight pounds of tomatoes four pounds of sugar a pint of vinegar, a teaspoonful of mace and one of cinnamon, half a teaspoon of cloves; boil till thick.

39

The Physical Director.

*

This department may with the greatest truth be affirmed to be worth double the Price of the Book, as the receipts are not only safe and cheap, but such as can be easily procured, and are what cannot possibly do the least harm to the constitution, if they should not have the desired effect, which I believe will very seldom or *never* happen.

To Break Up a Fresh Cold. Nothing is better than a glass of hot flip on going to bed. Put the poker in the fire to heat. Mix some ginger and molasses in a beer mug. Pour on some sour cider. Plunge in the red hot poker and stir it up till it foams well. This is a very agreeable cure. Warm the bed hot with the warming pan and put in some hot bricks. A fine sweat will carry off the cold.

A Quaker Stew is good for an inflamed throat and itching cough. Take a piece of butter the size of a shag bark, a pint of molasses, a little vinegar and a dash of red pepper. Boil until it strings. Take hot or cold in doses to suit.

A Slice of salt pork spread with black pepper and bound on with a strip of red flannel will cure a sore throat. Take brandy made thick with sugar, and a drop of camphor. Let this dissolve on the tongue.

"For a sudden attack of quinsy or croup bathe the neck with bear's grease and pour it down the throat. Goose grease or any kind of oily grease is as good as bear's grease."—*Mrs. Child.*

For a cold that is tight on the lungs, give hot ginger and sage tea to sweat. Onions stewed in molasses are loosening. Put draughts of wilted horseradish leaves on the feet. Put hen's oil or skunks oil over the chest and pack in hot flannels. A drop or two of hen's oil on a lump of sugar will loosen up a cold. If there is a pain in the side, put on a mustard paste.

FOR A COUGH. Boil a teacup of flaxseed in a quart of water, to a pint. Add a gill of molasses or honey, simmer ten minutes and cool, add a few drops of lemon juice.

FOR HUMORS IN THE BLOOD. Make a paste of sulphur, cream of tartar and molasses. Take a teaspoonful three mornings, skip three, take three.

SYRUP FOR THE SPRING OF THE YEAR. Boil together, dock root, thoroughwort, yarrow, mullein, sarsaparilla, coltsfoot, spearmint, May weed, dandelion root, and any other herbs you like. Boil down the water and add molasses to make a syrup. Put in brandy to keep. Make a good deal of this, and give all the family a tablespoonful before breakfast as a preventive of Spring fevers.

"ELIXIR PRO, is a useful family medicine for digestive disorders. Pulverize one ounce of saffron, one ounce of myrrh, one ounce aloes. Steep the myrrh in a half pint of brandy or N. E. rum for four days. Add the saffron and aloes; let it stand in the sunshine or a warm place for a fortnight, shaking it twice a day. Then fill up the bottle with brandy or N. E. rum. The longer it stands the better."—*Mrs. S. M. Child.*

"FOR AN ORDINARY HEADACHE take a shovel full of clean wood ashes; put them into clear cold water. When it has settled drink the water. It may cause vomiting; if it does the headache will be relieved the sooner."—*Mrs. E. A. Howland.*

"FOR EARACHE. Soak the feet in warm water; roast an onion and put the head of it into the ear as hot as can be borne; take the feet out of the water and bind roasted onions on them."
—*Mrs. Howland.*

"FOR DEAFNESS. Take a strong glass bottle, nearly fill it with clarified honey. Insert the bottle into the center of an

41

unbaked loaf of bread and bake thoroughly. Pour a small quantity of the honey into your ears and protect them from the external air with cotton."—*Mrs. Howland.*

"FOR HYDROPHOBIA. Wash oyster shells, put them on a bed of live coals and burn them thoroughly. Reduce to powder and sift through a fine sieve. Take three tablespoons of this powder add a sufficiency of egg to make a soft dough, and fry in in a little butter or olive oil. Let the patient eat this cake it the morning, and abstain from food or drink for six hours. This dose repeated for three mornings, is in all cases sufficient."

—*Mrs. Howland.*

A GOOD quantity of old cheese is the best thing to eat when distressed by eating too much fruit or oppressed with any kind of food.

AN OINTMENT made of ground worms rubbed on with the hand is excellent when the sinews are drawn up.

" ELDER BLOW TEA is peculiarly efficacious for babes or for grown people when the digestive powers are out of order."

Mrs. Child.

"MOTHERWORT is very quieting to the nerves. Students and wakeful people find it useful.—*Mrs. Child.*

PENNYROYAL is good for the cholic.

CAMOMILE FOR CONSUMPTION. "The attention of a young lady, apparently in the last stage of consumption, was called to the virtue of camomile, by observing from her window early each morning, a dog with scarcely any flesh on his bones go and lick the dew off a camomile bed in the garden, in doing which the animal was noticed to alter his appearance, to recover his strength, and finally looked plump and well. The singularity of the circumstance induced the lady to follow the dog's example. She procured dew from the same bed of camomile, drank a

42.

small quantity each morning and experienced relief. Her appetite became regular, she found a return of spirits, and in the end was completely cured."—*Mrs. Child*.

OTHER CURES FOR CONSUMPTION. Take no Food but new Buttermilk churned in a Bottle, and white Bread, I have known this successful.—Or, every Morning cut a little Turf of fresh Earth, and lying down breathe into the hole for a Quarter of an Hour. I have known a deep Consumption cured thus.

THE JAUNDICE. Take as much as will lie on a Shilling, of calcined Egg-Shell, three mornings fasting, and walk till you sweat.—Or half a Pint of Strong Decotion of Nettles.

THE KING'S EVIL. Take as much cream of Tartar as will lie on a Sixpence, every Morning and Evening.

FOR AN AGUE. Take a dram of Powder of Myrrh, mix it in a Spoonful of Sack, then take it and drink a glass of sack after it. Do this as near as possible, an hour before the fits come on.
—*Doctor Mead*.

A COLD IN THE HEAD. Pare very thin the yellow rhine of an orange; roll it up inside out and thrust a roll into each nostril.

FOR A BRUISE Apply a Plaister of chopped Parsley mixed with Butter.

FOR CHIN COUGH OR HOOPING COUGH. Rub the back at lying down with old Rum. It seldom fails.—Or give a spoonful of Juice of Penny-royal mixed with brown Sugar-Candy, twice a Day.

Food for the Sick.

❧

WINE WHEY. One pint of cream sweetened to your taste, warmed hot. Stir in sweet wine until curdled, grate in cinnamon and nutmeg.—*"Amer. Cook," 1808.*

A SICK BED CUSTARD. Scald a quart of milk, sweeten and salt it a little, whip three eggs and stir in. Bake on coals in a pewter vessel.—*Amer. Cook.*

MILK PORRIDGE. Boil new milk. Stir flour thoroughly into cold milk in a bowl, and pour it into the boiling milk. Let it cook six or eight minutes. Season with salt and if the patient likes with sugar and nutmeg.

DR. RATCLIFF'S RESTORATIVE PORK JELLY. Take a leg of well fed pork, beat it and break the bone. Set it over a gentle fire with three gallons of water, half an ounce each of mace and nutmeg and simmer it down to one gallon. Strain, cool and take off the fat. Give a cupful the first and last thing and at noon, putting salt to taste.

"CHICKEN PANADA. Boil the chicken in a quart of water. Take off the skin. Put the white meat when cold into a marble mortar. Pound it to a paste with a little of the broth. Season with salt, a grate of nutmeg, and the least bit of lemon peel. Boil gently a few minutes to the consistency you wish. It should be such as you can drink, though tolerably thick. This conveys great nourishment in small compass."
—*Lady from Phila. 1808.*

CAUDLE. Make a fine smooth gruel of half grits. Strain and cool, stir at times. When to be used, add sugar, wine, lemon peel, and nutmeg. Some like a spoonful of brandy beside.

"CAUDLE TO GIVE AWAY TO POOR FAMILIES. Set three quarts of water on the fire. Mix smooth, enough oatmeal to thicken it with a pint of water. Pour this into the boiling water with twenty powdered Jamaica peppers. Boil to a good middling thickness, then add sugar, half a pint of well fermented table beer and a glass of gin. Boil all."—*A Lady, Phila. 1808.*

Miscellany.

❦

SOAP MAKING. Save some weak lye when you make soap and put it in the soap-grease barrel down cellar. Drop into it all your bacon rinds, bits of fat meat, the top of the pot after boiling salt meat, your cake fat when it gets dark, and everything fat that comes along. It is amazing how much comes along in the course of a year. The lye will work on it and keep it.

In the spring when the ash hole is cleared have five or six bushels of ashes put in the ash leach, if you have one; if not a hogshead, with holes bored in the bottom, set up on sticks will do. Pour on enough water to wet the ashes thoroughly, but not to drip, and let them stand several days. Then pour on boiling water and let it drip into a tub. Continue putting on water until the lye grows weak. If it is strong enough to bear up an egg so that you can see a piece as big as a ninepence, it is about right.

On soap day morning get breakfast out of the way early and plan an easy dinner. Swing the six pail kettle on the crane for the soap, and a smaller one for the grease which should be put on to heat with some strong lye. As it dissolves dip it off into the big pot and add more lye and water. A little experience will teach how much of each. Too much lye will make it thin, and the soap will eat your clothes and your hands. Water will make it jell, but don't use too much or it will not keep. Boil until it becomes thick and ropy.

If it does not "come," take out a little in a dish and try first water, then lye and then grease until it does thicken. Then add to the big pot whatever seems needed and boil again. When it comes, empty the kettle and start again.

This is a good job done.—*Compiled*.

☞Making soap in the new of the moon may make no difference in its coming, but it certainly does no harm.

"OF CLEAR STARCHING. Take your Muslin aprons, Hoods, Neckcloths, fold them four double, putting the two Selvages together, then the ends together and wash it the way the Selvage goes; then take clear water, not too hot for that makes them yellow, and strain the water through a cloth; Take a small Quantity of the best soap, put it upon a clean Stick and beat up your lather; let it not be with a whisk because it will make the water yellow.

Let your Muslins stand to soak, then wash them one by one, squeeze them, and shake them open into a dish; then let your Second Lather be beat up as your first only hotter, but not Scalding. Wash whilst they are warm and squeeze as before; as to the third Lather let the Water be scalding, but not boiling, for that makes the water yellow. * * * To rinse them take Pump water in a clean pan with a small quantity of Powder Blue. * * * Squeeze them very hard and pull them out with dry Hands. * * * *

To Starch. Take a Pint of Pump water to a Quarter of a Pound of Starch, put the Water in a Skillet, and put it over a

46

clear Fire till it is lukewarm, then put in your Starch, keep it stirring one Way till it boils, one Boil and no more; when it is cold, take some upon your hand, and some Blue in the other Hand, and mix them together, but make it not too blue; take your muslins doubled as before one by one, then spread the starch with your Hand but not too thick, first on one side and then the other, but not open it; * * when you have starched the Muslins, lay them in an earthen Dish, Kneading them with your double Fist, till the starch sticks about your Hands, then Squeezing them hard wipe them with a dry cloth; open them, rub them slightly through your Hands; take the two Ends, and so clap them between your Hands; hold them against the Light to See if they are clapped enough. If any Thing looks shining, that is the Starch, you might rub it over gently; when they are clapped enough you will observe them to fly asunder, and not stick to your hands; but observe to clap very thick and very hard, for if you let them dry they will be limber. You must never clap them single, for that frays and tears them; neither clap by the Fire, except in frosty weather, for that spoils the Colour.

For the ironing of Muslins, pull them out double on the Board, as smooth and even as you can, and so on till you finish about six one upon another; then with your Box-iron, iron the under one first, because it is the driest. Let fine plain muslin be ironed upon a soft woolen cloth. * * * *

A whole Book might be written on the Art of clear starching, but all the Directions in the World cannot make a Skilled Starcher. It can only be learned by years of labour.

SPRUCE BEER. For a half barrel kag, take a good sized bunch of spruce and birch twigs, a little princess piney, some checkerberry leaves, a few rings of dried pumpkin, a good handful of hops, some malt or bran, or both, and anything else you like. Boil them all together in the big pot until the taste is

47

well out. Strain off the liquor, add a quart or two of molasses and a pint of emptins. Pour it into the beer keg and let it work a day or two before using. It will keep a week or two Save some of the emptins in the bottom of the keg to raise the next.—*Compiled.*

BLACKBERRY WINE. Jam the berries and let them stand twelve hours. Strain and add three pounds sugar to three quarts juice; let it stand twenty-four hours. Add water enough to make a gallon. Do not close it tight until it is done fermenting, then cork up.

All kinds of berry wine can be made the same way, except that currants require four pounds of sugar to a gallon of juice and water.

RASPBERRY VINEGAR. Pour three pints vinegar over one and a half pints raspberries. Let it stand twenty-four hours. Then strain the liquor over another one and a half pint of berries and let it stand twenty-four hours. Repeat this the third day. Drain off the vinegar through a jelly bag without squeezing, into a stone jar. To every pint of liquor put one pound of pounded loaf sugar. When sugar is disolved cover the jar and set it in a saucepan of boiling water. Boil an hour, skimming often. When cold bottle. Use no metal vessel in doing this. A large spoonful in a glass of water makes a refreshing beverage, good for colds or fevers.—*Mrs. Solly.*

CANDLE DIPPING. The young girls in the family who are learning to spin can practice on the candle wicking. Keep a supply on hand by having them do it at odd times. Tow does very well for common candles. Buy a little cotton for the best ones. Cut the wicking by winding it around a board of the proper length, and running a sharp knife across the end. Put six wicks on each candle rod, doubling and twirling each one. Dip them in alum water to keep the candles from running.

48

Place two long poles across the kitchen a foot or more apart, resting the ends on chair backs at a convenient height from the floor, and put an old board under them to catch the drips. Melt the tallow in a brass kettle and set on the floor. Take the rods one at a time and dip the wicks in the hot tallow, Before they cool and stiffen, straighten each wick carfully and pinch the end close. Any carelessness in this first dip will make a crooked candle. If they hang straight and at even distances on the rods, the whole dripping is made easy. Rest the rod across the poles. When you have gone through all the rods, the first ones will be cool enough to begin again. Take two rods this time in your right hand, with the forefinger between to keep them apart. Dip the wicks in with a quick slanting motion, letting them stay just long enough to take a coating of tallow, but not long enough to melt the first coat. Keep the kettle full and hot by pouring in boiling water as the tallow lowers. If it grows cool the candles will make faster but will be rough and uneven. Two dozen dippings ought to make them as large as an ordinary candle stick requires. Let them harden thoroughly before you slip them from the rods. Bees wax melted in the tallow makes them harden. Bleach some of the best ones by hanging them in the window when the sun will strike them.

⌐ If you wish to make only a few run them in molds.

POTATO STARCH. Peel and grate a quantity of potatoes; put the pulp into a coarse cloth between two boards and press it dry. Mix the juice with an equal quantity of water. In an hour's time it will deposit a fine sediment, on which pour boiling water, and your starch is ready for use. Or dry the sediment in the sun and keep for future use.

SKIMMED MILK is a good starch for calicoes.

—*Economical Housekeeper.*

SUBSTITUTES FOR TEA AND COFFEE. The leaves of currant bushes picked very small and dried on tin can hardly be distinguished from green tea. Peas roasted and ground are an excellent substitute for coffee and you would hardly know which was best.—*Economical Housekeeper*.

SAVE all your fish skin, wash and dry it and keep to settle coffee.

SHOE BLACKING. Wash elderberries in a kettle of water. Set them in the shade for a day or two to ferment, then boil it half a day, adding a little water as needed. Strain the liquid and boil it down to the thickness of molasses. It will give a fine gloss with rubbing.—*Economical Housekeeper*.

GOOD WRITING INK can be made the same way.

TO PREVENT FLIES FROM INJURING PICTURE FRAMES, ETC. Boil three or four onions in a pint of water; then with a gilding brush do over your pictures and frames. The flies will not light on them. This may be used without apprehension, as it will not do the least injury to the frames.—*Ecoonmical Housekeeper*.

ROSE WATER. Pick rose leaves when they are in full blossom. Put a peck of them to a quart of water in a cold still over a slow fire and distill very gradually. Bottle the water, let it stand three days and cork it close.

TO PRESERVE SWEET FLAG. Scrape and wash the flag root and cut it in thin slices. Boil until it is tender. Make a thick syrup of sugar and water and boil the flag in it until it candies. Spread it out to dry.

DRY SWEET FLAG-ROOT. Grated and mixed with sugar it cures colic in babies.

Dyes.

***

PURPLE SLATE. Boil the paper that comes around loaf sugar in cider in an iron pot. Set with alum.

NANKEEN. A piece of copperas half as big as a hen's egg in a pail of lye will make a color that will never wash out. Useful to line bedquilts. Old faded gowns can be colored and made into petticoats.

STRAW COLOR. Saffron steeped in earthen and strained.

BIRD OF PARADISE COLOR. Dry the outside skin of onions, and steep in scalding water.

DARK SLATE. Boil maple leaves, set with alum.

BROWN. Boil butternuts. Set with alum.

R. A. RICHARDS, D. D. S.,
DENTIST,

Botsford's Block, 51 Main Street,

GREENFIELD, MASS.

❧

Office Hours: 8.30 to 12 A. M. 1 to 5.30 P. M.

❧

Crown and Bridge Work a Specialty.

When you are following the directions for cooking given in this book perchance you may find that some of your extracts are low. If so, the White Pharmacy invite you to try theirs for they are the best. In bringing your Prescriptions to us you get the best goods obtainable correctly dispensed.

THE WHITE PHARMACY,

55 Main Street, GREENFIELD, MASS.

THE GEO. H. HOVEY PHARMACY,

HENRY C. WILLARD, MGR.

Prescription Specialists, and Family Chemists.

GREENFIELD, MASS.

WINN & GRISWOLD,

Attorneys at Law,

Rooms 2, 3 and 4, Pond's Block, Main Street,

GREENFIELD, MASS.

The Pocumtuc Housewife,

PUBLISHED BY THE WILLARD
LEND - A - HAND SOCIETY OF
DEERFIELD, MASS. . . .

Price 50 cts.

Copies may be had of Miss Jane Pratt,
Miss Margaret Miller or Miss Mary
E. Allen of Deerfield.

●

Done at Ye Print Shop
of John C. Otto,
Springfield

www.ingramcontent.com/pod-product-compliance
Lightning Source LLC
Chambersburg PA
CBHW021627270326
41931CB00008B/899